Covered Calls

How to Generate High Yields Using an Options Trading Strategy

Preface

Are you sick of watching your portfolio swing wildly with the market?

Do you dream of a steady, reliable investment income, regardless of the economic climate?

What if a simple, powerful strategy could help you achieve both?

The answer is "Covered Calls." This underrated gem in the options trading world has the potential to transform your financial future. But where do you begin? Fear not, for "Covered Calls" is your ultimate guide to unlocking this remarkable strategy, even if you're a complete beginner.

"Covered Calls" is your roadmap to financial freedom. It's your chance to break free from the market's volatility and unlock the potential of a powerful, income-generating strategy.

Table of Contents

Introduction

Do you yearn for consistent returns on your investments? Are you tired of meager dividends and unpredictable market swings? If so, then "Covered Calls" might be the key you've been searching for. This book, designed specifically for beginners, unveils a powerful options strategy that generates regular income while protecting your capital, even in volatile markets.

Isn't options trading complex and risky? Not necessarily. When implemented correctly, covered calls provide a structured and approachable way to tap into the options market. This book takes you by the hand, guiding you through every step of the process, from understanding the basic mechanics to crafting and executing your covered call strategies.

Here's what sets "Covered Calls" apart:

- **Crystal-Clear Explanations:** Forget jargon-filled prose! This book breaks down complex concepts into easy-to-understand language, making it accessible even for those without experience.
- **Step-by-Step Guidance:** Each chapter is like a roadmap, leading you from fundamental principles to practical application. You'll gain the confidence to navigate the options market with clear, actionable steps.
- **Hands-on Approach:** Theory is great, but practice makes perfect. The book provides real-world examples, case studies, and

actionable exercises to help you solidify your understanding and build your trading skills.

- **Risk Management Focus:** Mitigating risk is paramount. This book equips you with the tools and knowledge to identify and manage potential risks, ensuring you approach covered calls with a prudent and informed perspective.
- **Beyond the Basics:** While starting strong is crucial, the book doesn't stop there. It delves into advanced strategies and considerations, preparing you to take your covered call journey to the next level.

Whether you're a seasoned investor or just starting, "Covered Calls" offers a valuable roadmap to unlocking the potential of this powerful strategy. It's your chance to:

- **Consistent Income:** Generate regular option premiums, turning your portfolio into an income-generating machine.
- **Downside Protection:** Shield your investments from market downturns, sleeping soundly, knowing your capital is safeguarded.
- **Market Resilience:** Navigate volatility with confidence and composure, unfazed by the market's unpredictable swings.
- **Newfound Skill:** Expand your investment horizons and gain a valuable skill that can benefit you for years.

Don't let fear or uncertainty hold you back. Take control of your financial future with "Covered Calls." Open this book and unlock options-based income generation.

The first step is always the most important. Don't wait any longer to embark on your covered call journey. Start reading today and unlock the potential for consistent returns and a more secure financial future.

Chapter 1

Understanding Options Trading

Forget the stock market rollercoasters. There's an entirely different world beyond the traditional buy-and-hold of shares and bonds. Welcome to options trading, where informed speculation meets strategic flexibility. It offers opportunities for potential profit beyond the limitations of static investments.

For many investors, options trading conjures images of Wall Street wolves and risky bets. However, beneath the surface lies a versatile tool capable of enhancing your investment strategies and generating income in ways traditional stocks and bonds cannot. This chapter is your gateway to understanding options, their nuances, and the potential they hold.

Basics of Options Trading

The well-trodden path of stocks and bonds feels familiar, like a comfortable pair of shoes. However, what if there's an exciting alleyway just around the corner, beckoning with the promise of amplified returns and strategic income generation? That's options trading, and while it might seem intimidating at first glance, understanding it in detail will unlock a treasure trove of possibilities.

Here is a table for the Key Differences: Options vs. Stocks vs. Bonds:

Feature	Stocks	Bonds	Options
Ownership	Direct ownership of a share	Lend money to the issuer, earn interest	No ownership, right to buy or sell
Obligation	No obligation to sell	No obligation to buy back before maturity	Option to exercise or let expire
Price Movement	Profits/losses based on share price movement	Profits/losses based on interest rate changes and price fluctuations	Profits/losses based on price difference, strike price, and time decay
Complexity	Relatively straightforward	More complex due to interest rate dynamics	More complex due to contract terms, strategies, and risk factors
Return Potential	Limited to price appreciation (plus dividends)	Limited to interest payments and potential price appreciation	High potential for profits and losses, depending on the strategy

Contracts and the Power of Leverage

Unlike stocks and bonds, where you directly own a piece of the pie, options are contracts granting you the right, not the obligation, to buy or sell an underlying asset (like a stock) at a specific price by a certain date. It's a temporary claim on the asset, not a permanent deed. This key difference unlocks unique advantages:

- **Limited vs. Unlimited Potential:** With stocks, your potential gains are theoretically limitless, but losses are capped at your investment. Options, however, involve defined risk. Your premium for the contract is your maximum loss, while potential gains can be significantly amplified. Suppose you buy a call option on a stock you believe will soar. If your prediction is right, you will leverage your initial investment to control a much larger stake in the stock's appreciation.

- **Flexibility and Strategic Income:** Options offer a broader spectrum of strategies than traditional investments. You use them to speculate on price movements, hedge existing holdings, or even generate income through strategies like covered calls (selling calls against owned stock). This flexibility allows you to tailor your investment approach to your specific goals and risk tolerance.

Call vs. Put

Options have two sides: call options and put options. Each empowers you to make a directional bet on the underlying asset's price movement:

- **Call Options:** When you're convinced a stock is about to take off, a call option gives you the right to buy the stock at a specific price (strike price) by a certain date (expiry). If your prediction holds, you exercise the option and purchase the stock at the lower strike price, pocketing the difference. It's like buying a discounted ticket to a concert you know will be amazing.

- **Put Options:** Conversely, if you foresee a stock plummeting, a put option gives you the right to sell the stock at the strike price by expiry. If your bearish intuition is correct, you exercise the option and sell the stock at the higher strike price, profiting from the price decline. It's an insurance policy against a potential market downturn.

Beyond Basic Strategies

Options aren't just binary bets. They offer a toolbox of strategies to operate in various market scenarios:

- **Bullish Strategies:** Soaring markets call for bullish strategies like buying calls directly or using spreads (combining calls and puts) for defined risk and income generation. Covered calls, where you sell calls against owned stock, are also a powerful tool for income generation in a rising market.

- **Bearish Strategies:** When the market seems headed south, you call on bearish strategies like buying puts directly, using protective puts to safeguard your existing stock positions, or even implementing credit spreads (selling options for income) with defined risk.

- **Neutral Strategies:** Flat markets don't have to mean stagnant returns. Options offer neutral strategies like selling covered calls for income, using iron condors (combining multiple calls and puts) for defined risk and income, or employing calendar spreads (using options with different expiry dates) for directional bets.

Risk Management in Options

While options offer exciting potential, they also come with inherent risks. Before venturing into this domain, remember:

- **Volatility Is a Double-Edged Sword:** Fluctuations in the underlying asset's price significantly impact option prices and your potential gains/losses. Understand how volatility works and factor it into your strategies.

- **Time Is Money (Literally):** Options lose value as they approach expiry, regardless of the underlying asset's price movement. Be mindful of expiry dates and potential time-based losses.

- **Liquidity Matters:** Ensure sufficient trading volume in your chosen options for easy entry and exit. Illiquid options are harder to trade and involve wider bid-ask spreads, impacting your returns.

- **Discipline Is Your Compass:** Start small, set clear profit and loss targets, and stick to your trading plan. Options are powerful tools but require responsible use and a healthy dose of discipline.

Bulls, Bears, and Beyond

The market, like the weather, is notoriously unpredictable. However, unlike the weather, you can prepare for its fluctuations and turn them to your advantage using options strategies. Whether the market is charging like a bull, sulking like a bear, or just chilling neutrally, there's a strategy out there waiting to be your financial umbrella.

Bullish Whispers? Embrace the Horns with These Strategies:

- **Buying Calls:** This is the classic "go long" approach. You directly buy the right to buy an asset at a specific price (strike price) by a certain date. If the market soars past that strike price, you exercise your option and pocket the difference, potentially amplifying your gains.

- **Bullish Spreads:** Want to define your risk while still enjoying the potential for amplified gains? Bullish spreads combine calls and puts, creating a safety net while allowing you to profit from a bullish market. It's a built-in insurance policy for your optimism.

- **Covered Calls:** Already own some stock and want to generate some income while you wait for it to appreciate? Covered calls are your friend. You sell calls against your existing shares, collecting a premium upfront. If the stock stays below the strike price, you keep the premium and your shares. If it rises above, you sell your shares at the strike price (still profiting from your initial purchase). It's like renting out a spare room while waiting for the perfect buyer.

Are Bearish Clouds Looming? Don't Despair, These Strategies Will Help You Weather the Storm:

- **Buying Puts:** The opposite of buying calls, this strategy lets you profit from a price decline. You buy the right to sell an asset at a specific price by a certain date. If the market tanks, you exercise your option and sell at the higher strike price, pocketing the difference.

- **Bearish Spreads:** Just like bullish spreads offer defined risk in a rising market, bearish spreads do the same in a falling market. By using put combinations, you can limit your potential losses while still profiting from a downturn.

- **Protective Puts:** Worried about your existing stock positions in a potentially bearish market? Protective puts act as a safety net. You buy puts on your stocks, giving you the right to sell them at a specific price if things go south. It's a backup plan in case your initial investment gets caught in the downward trends.

Market Chilling? Don't Get Left Out in the Cold, Try These Neutral Strategies:

- **Selling Covered Calls:** Even in a sideways market, you can generate income. By selling covered calls on stocks you own, you collect a premium upfront. If the stock stays within a certain range (determined by the strike price), you keep both the premium and your shares.

- **Iron Condors:** This advanced strategy uses multiple calls and puts to create a defined risk and income zone. It's like setting up a trading tent with clear boundaries, allowing you to collect premiums while limiting your potential losses.

- **Calendar Spreads:** Want to make a directional bet on the market with limited risk? Calendar spreads use options with different expiry dates to achieve this. It's two weather forecasts, one for the near future and one for the long term, helping you make informed decisions based on both.

These are just a few examples. The world of options is vast, and there are strategies for every market condition and risk tolerance. Do your research, understand the risks, and start small before diving in. With the right knowledge and strategy, you will navigate the market's ups and downs like a seasoned pro, turning every scenario into an opportunity.

Risk and Reward: A Prerequisite for Options Exploration

Like any financial venture, options trading is a captivating dance between potential reward and inherent risk. Understanding this delicate partnership is crucial before delving into the intricacies of covered calls. It's time to explore the complexities of risk and reward in the options arena.

The Risk Side of the Coin:

Options are not without their risks. Here are some key aspects to consider:

- **Premium Payment:** Unlike stocks, where your loss is limited to your investment, options involve an upfront premium cost. It's the price you pay for the contract, representing your maximum loss if the option expires worthless.
- **Time Decay:** Options are perishable assets. Their value steadily declines as they approach their expiry date, regardless of the underlying asset's price movement. This "time decay" adds another layer of risk to your trade.
- **Volatility's Wild Card:** The market's volatility significantly impacts options prices. High volatility leads to rapid price swings, amplifying both your potential gains and losses. Understanding volatility and its impact is crucial for informed trading.
- **Leverage's Double-Edged Sword:** Options offer leverage, allowing you to control a larger position in the underlying asset with a smaller investment. It magnifies your profits but also magnifies your losses. Handle leverage with caution and discipline.

The Reward Side of the Equation:

Now, it's time to look at the alluring side of the coin, the potential rewards:

- **Amplified Gains:** Unlike stocks, where your profit is capped at the difference between your purchase price and the selling price, options offer the potential for unlimited gains. If your prediction about the underlying asset's price movement is correct, the profits will significantly exceed your initial investment.

- **Defined Risk:** Unlike buying a stock where your losses are theoretically unlimited, options have defined risk. Your maximum loss is limited to the premium you paid for the contract, which gives you a level of control and protection not found in tradigtional investments.

- **Income Generation:** Options offer various strategies like covered calls that generate income even in flat or sideways markets. This income supplements your returns and potentially offsets losses in other parts of your portfolio.

Balancing the Scales: Risk Management Is Key

Before diving into options, remember that risk management is paramount. Always:

- **Start Small:** Don't risk a significant portion of your capital initially. Gain experience and confidence before increasing your position.

- **Set Stop-Loss Orders:** Limit your potential losses by setting stop-loss orders that automatically exit your trade when the option reaches a certain price point.

- **Understand Your Risk Tolerance:** Be honest with yourself about how much risk you're comfortable with and stick to strategies that match your risk profile.

- **Do Your Research:** Thoroughly research the underlying asset, the option you're considering, and the market conditions before making a trade.

Now that you've demystified the basic concepts of options, you stand on a solid foundation. You understand the difference between calls and puts, glimpse the potential of different strategies, and gain a healthy respect for the inherent risks. The journey of mastering options trading is a continuous learning process. Don't be discouraged by initial complexities. Use them as fuel for further exploration. As you dive deeper into the chapters ahead, you'll discover how covered calls utilize these core concepts to generate potential income while mitigating risk. Stay curious, stay engaged, and prepare to unlock the power of covered calls.

Chapter 2

Basics of Covered Calls

With its diverse strategies and potential for amplified returns, the options market can be a tantalizing yet daunting landscape for investors. In this chapter, you'll unlock the secrets of a fundamental option strategy, the covered call.

More than just a fancy name, covered calls offer a blend of income generation and downside protection. You'll be earning cash while simultaneously safeguarding your existing stock positions. Sounds too good to be true? Buckle up because it's time to understand the mechanics, benefits, and risks of this versatile strategy.

Through clear explanations, real-world examples, and practical tips, you'll be equipped with the knowledge and confidence to navigate covered calls with ease. Whether you're a seasoned options veteran or a curious newcomer, this chapter promises to be your essential guide to mastering this powerful tool in your trading arsenal.

Income Generation with a Safety Net

Covered calls are a strategy that generates consistent income while protecting your investments. If you're curious about options trading but intimidated by its complexity, covered calls might be the perfect entry point. It's time to demystify this strategy and see if it fits your investment goals.

What Is a Covered Call?

A covered call is a double-edged sword, offering both income and protection. On one hand, you sell a call option on an underlying asset (like a stock) you already own. It grants the buyer the right, but not the obligation, to buy the asset from you at a specific price (strike price) by a certain date (expiration date). In return, you receive an upfront premium, essentially renting out your potential upside in exchange for immediate income.

Key Differences from Uncovered Calls

Unlike its riskier cousin, the uncovered call, where you sell an option without owning the underlying asset, a covered call involves owning the shares you're selling calls against. It provides a safety net. If the buyer exercises the option, you simply deliver the shares you already own.

Mechanics Breakdown:

- **Underlying Asset:** This is the stock, ETF, or other security you hold and sell calls against. Choose an asset you believe will either stay flat or experience moderate growth.
- **Call Options:** These contracts give the buyer the right to buy your shares at the strike price by the expiration date. You set the strike price and expiration based on your risk tolerance and income goals.
- **Strike Price:** This is the predetermined price at which the buyer purchases your shares if they exercise the option. Choose a strike price that aligns with your expectations for the asset's price movement.

- **Expiration Date:** This is the deadline by which the option can be exercised. Options closer to expiry are cheaper but offer less time for potential price appreciation.
- **Premium:** This is the cash you receive upfront for selling the call option. It represents your income, regardless of whether the option is exercised or expires worthless.
- **Obligation to Sell:** If the buyer exercises the option, you must sell your shares at the strike price, even if the market price is higher. It limits your potential upside but provides downside protection.

Real-World Application

What's a better way to understand something than a real-life example? You own 100 shares of a stock trading at $50. You sell a covered call with a strike price of $55 and an expiration date in three months, collecting a premium of $2 per share. Here's how things will unfold:

- **Scenario 1: Stock Price Stays Flat or Falls Below $55:** The option expires worthless, and you keep both the premium and your shares. You've earned income without risking your initial investment.
- **Scenario 2: Stock Price Rises Above $55:** The buyer exercises the option, and you sell your shares at $55, pocketing a profit of $5 per share (excluding the premium). It limits your potential gains if the stock price soars beyond $55.

With careful planning and execution, the covered call can be a valuable tool for generating income and protecting your portfolio, allowing you to navigate the market with confidence and dance to the beat of your own financial goals.

Decoding the Payoffs

Covered calls, often shrouded in mystery, are a unique blend of income generation and potential capital gains. However, before you dive in, it's crucial to understand the payoffs. They include the potential rewards and risks associated with this strategy.

Profit Potential: Double Dipping into Gains

Covered calls are a two-pronged fork, spearing profits in two ways:

- **Premium Income:** The initial charm of covered calls lies in the premium, a sum of money you receive upfront for selling the call option. You get paid to rent out a portion of your investment, regardless of what happens to the underlying asset's price.

- **Capital Gains (Up to the Strike Price):** If the asset's price rises but stays below the strike price you set for the call option, you get to keep both the premium and the capital appreciation up to the strike price. If you sell calls on a stock that climbs from $50 to $54, you keep the premium and the $4 per share gain for a total profit of $6 per share.

Risk Profile: The Flip Side of the Coin

While covered calls offer potential profits, there's no such thing as a free lunch in the investment world:

- **Capped Upside:** The biggest trade-off is the limited upside potential. If the asset's price skyrockets beyond the strike price, you miss out on those additional gains. It's a price ceiling for your profits. Even if the stock reaches $60, you're still obligated to sell at $55 if the option is exercised.

- **Assignment Risk:** If the price rises above the strike price by the expiry date, the buyer has the right to exercise the option, forcing you to sell your shares at the strike price. It's frustrating if you believe the price will keep climbing.

Break-even Point: Finding Your Sweet Spot

So, when does a covered call make you money? The answer lies in the break-even point, which considers both the premium received and the strike price. Here's the formula:

Break-even Price = Strike Price - Premium Received

For instance, if you sell a call option with a strike price of $55 and collect a premium of $2 per share, your break-even point is $53 ($55 - $2). It means you only start making a profit if the asset's price stays above $53 by the expiry date.

Risk Management in the Driver's Seat

Covered calls offer alluring benefits, such as steady income, downside protection, and strategic flexibility. However, like any vehicle, understanding the controls is essential for a smooth and safe ride.

Strike Price Selection

The strike price is the limit you set for your covered call. Choosing wisely helps manage risk and align with your goals:

- **Risk Tolerance:** Prefer safety? Choose a strike price above the current market price, reducing your chances of assignment but also lowering your premium income. More comfortable with risk? Opt for a closer strike price for higher premiums, but be prepared for potential early assignment.

- **Desired Income:** Need immediate cash flow? Prioritize higher premiums by selecting a strike price closer to the current market price. Willing to wait for potential capital appreciation? Choose a higher strike price for lower premiums but allow room for the asset to rise.
- **Underlying Asset Volatility:** Highly volatile assets experience wider price swings, impacting your strike price selection. Consider setting a wider strike range to account for potential fluctuations, potentially sacrificing some premium income for safety.

Understanding Expiration Date

The expiration date acts like your destination on the covered call journey. Choosing wisely optimizes both risk and potential return:

- **Premium Decay:** Options lose value over time (time decay) like a ticking clock. Shorter expiry dates offer higher premiums but magnify time decay risk. Longer expirations provide more time for potential price appreciation but come with lower premiums.
- **Underlying Asset Volatility:** Highly volatile assets benefit from longer expirations, allowing more time for price movements to align with your chosen strike price. Less volatile assets can work well with shorter expirations, minimizing time decay concerns.

Volatility's Impact

The underlying asset's volatility is your constant companion on the covered call journey. Here's how it affects your ride:

- **Higher Volatility:** Increased volatility translates to wider price swings. It's risky with covered calls, as the asset might unexpectedly reach your strike price, leading to early assignment and missed upside potential.

- **Lower Volatility:** Lower volatility generally indicates smaller price movements. It provides more predictability and reduces the risk of early assignment, but it also limits your potential premium income.

Hedging Strategies

While covered calls offer downside protection, unforeseen circumstances can still cause turbulence. Consider these potential **hedging strategies** for additional security:

- **Protective Puts:** Buying a put option at a strike price below your break-even point creates a safety net. If the asset price plummets, you can exercise the put to sell it at a predetermined price, limiting your losses.
- **Collars:** This involves selling a covered call and simultaneously buying a protective put at a higher strike price. It combines income generation with downside protection but reduces your potential upside compared to a naked call.

Risk management is not a destination but an ongoing journey in covered call strategies. By understanding the above factors, you'll make informed decisions, adjust your approach as needed, and navigate the financial landscape with confidence. Get behind the wheel, manage your risks wisely, and enjoy the rewarding ride that covered calls offer.

Practical Insights for Traders

Covered calls, with their blend of income generation and downside protection, are a valuable tool for traders. However, before hitting the "buy" button, it's time to equip you with some practical insights to navigate this strategy effectively.

Identifying Suitable Assets

Not every asset is created equal for covered calls. Look for these characteristics:

- **Liquidity:** Ensure sufficient trading volume in both the underlying asset and the options contracts for easy entry and exit. Low liquidity widens bid-ask spreads and impacts your returns.
- **Volatility:** Moderate volatility is a sweet spot. Highly volatile assets increase the risk of early assignment, while low volatility might limit your premium income. Consider your risk tolerance when selecting.
- **Dividend Yield:** If you plan to hold the asset long-term, choose stocks with healthy dividend yields. You receive both the premium and the dividend, boosting your overall return.

Order Placement and Monitoring

Placing a covered call involves two orders:

- **Buying the Underlying Asset:** Ensure you own the shares before selling the call option.
- **Selling the Call Option:** Specify the strike price, expiration date, and quantity of contracts. Monitor your position regularly, tracking the asset price, option premium, and your break-even point.

Curbing Early Assignment

Early assignments can disrupt your plans. Here are some strategies:

- **Rolling the Option:** Close out your existing call option and sell a new one with a higher strike price and further expiry date. It reduces the immediate assignment risk but lowers your premium income.

- **Adjusting Strike Prices:** Choose wider strike price ranges when initially selling the call, providing more buffer against unexpected price movements.

Tax Time Considerations

Remember, covered calls have tax implications:

- **Premium Income:** The premiums you receive are considered taxable income in the year you receive them.
- **Capital Gains/Losses:** When you sell the underlying asset, you realize capital gains or losses based on the difference between your purchase and selling prices (including assignment).

Covered calls are powerful but require planning and ongoing management. By following these practical insights, you'll make informed decisions, choose suitable assets, manage risks effectively, and deal with the tax implications confidently.

Covered Call Case Study: Putting Theory into Practice

Prepare to take the theoretical knowledge from the previous sections and apply it to a real-world example of a covered call trade. You own 100 shares of Apple (AAPL) stock, currently trading at $150 per share. You believe the stock may experience moderate price appreciation but are unsure about significant upward movement. You decide to use a covered call to generate some income while limiting your downside risk.

Choosing the Strike Price and Expiration

Considering your goals and current market conditions, you opt for the following:

- **Strike Price:** $160. It provides a buffer for potential price increases while still offering a decent premium.
- **Expiration Date:** Three months from now. It balances time decay with the possibility of price movement.

Selling the Call Option

You find a buyer willing to purchase the call option with your chosen strike price and expiration date for a premium of $4 per share. You receive $400 upfront ($4 x 100 shares).

Potential Outcomes

Scenario 1: Stock Price Stays Below $160 by Expiration:

- The option expires worthless, and you keep both the premium ($400) and your 100 shares of AAPL. You've effectively earned a 2.67% return on your investment (considering the $400 premium over the $15,000 cost of the shares) in 3 months, regardless of the stock price movement.

Scenario 2: Stock Price Rises Above $160 by Expiration:

- The call option is exercised, and you are obligated to sell your 100 shares of AAPL at the strike price of $160 each. You earn a total of $16,000 ($160 x 100 shares) for your shares, plus the initial premium of $400, resulting in a total profit of $1,000 or a 6.67% return on your investment (excluding commissions and potential taxes). However, you miss out on any further gains if the stock price continues to rise beyond $160.

This is just a simplified example, and actual results may vary due to factors like commissions, taxes, and unexpected market movements.

Additional Notes:

- You can use online options calculators to estimate potential returns and break-even points for various strike prices and expiration dates.
- Consider transaction costs like commissions and spreads when calculating your final returns.
- Always conduct your research and understand the risks involved before entering any trade.

As you conclude your exploration of covered calls, remember that they are not a magic bullet but rather a strategic tool requiring careful planning and execution. Understanding the concepts discussed in this chapter gives you a solid foundation to make informed decisions.

Armed with this knowledge, you can:

- Identify suitable assets for covered calls based on their characteristics.
- Choose appropriate strike prices and expiration dates to align with your risk tolerance and goals.
- Monitor your positions and adjust your strategy as needed.
- Manage potential risks associated with covered calls, such as early assignments.

The options market offers endless possibilities, and covered calls are just one piece of the puzzle. As you continue your journey, keep exploring, learning, and adapting your strategies to your unique investment goals. With dedication and a thirst for knowledge, you will unlock the full potential of covered calls and become a master of this rewarding option strategy.

Chapter 3

Selecting the Right Stocks

Welcome to Chapter 3, the pivotal point in your covered call journey. While understanding the mechanics is crucial, the stock you choose ultimately dictates your success. This chapter equips you with the essential knowledge and tools to identify your perfect match, a stock that fits seamlessly with your goals and risk tolerance.

You'll discover the key characteristics that make a stock suitable for covered calls, exploring liquidity, volatility, and dividend considerations. You'll learn to navigate the intricate dance of maximizing income potential while managing risk through strategic selection.

Choosing the right stock isn't just about numbers and charts. You'll also explore the industry landscape, identifying sectors with promising potential and analyzing how company fundamentals contribute to a well-rounded selection. By the end of this chapter, you'll confidently navigate the vast stock market, transforming informed selection into a powerful tool for unlocking the full potential of covered calls.

Why Stock Selection Is the Heart of Covered Call Success

When it comes to covered calls, stock selection isn't just a step. It's the foundation upon which success hinges. While the mechanics of covered calls offer income generation and risk management potential, it's the underlying asset you choose that ultimately determines your profitability and risk exposure. Here's why selecting the right stock is paramount:

Maximizing Profits:

- **Premium Potential:** Different stocks offer varying premium levels based on factors like volatility and dividend yield. Choosing a stock with higher income-generating potential while managing risk directly impacts your overall returns.

- **Capital Appreciation:** While covered calls limit your upside potential, selecting a stock with solid growth prospects benefits you from both premiums and potential price appreciation within your chosen strike range.

Managing Risks:

- **Early Assignment:** Choosing a stable stock with moderate volatility reduces the risk of early assignment, ensuring you hold the shares long enough to collect the desired premium.

- **Downside Protection:** Selecting a stock with strong fundamentals and long-term potential helps mitigate potential losses even if the price dips below your strike price.

- **Volatility:** Understanding the underlying asset's volatility allows you to set appropriate strike prices and expirations, minimizing the impact of unexpected price swings.

Beyond the Basics:

- **Industry Trends:** Aligning your stock selection with positive industry trends increases the likelihood of capital appreciation, boosting overall returns.

- **Dividend Considerations:** Choosing dividend-paying stocks adds another income layer to your covered call strategy.
- **Personal Preferences:** Tailoring your selection to your risk tolerance and investment goals ensures a comfortable and aligned approach.

Stock selection is an ongoing process that requires research, analysis, and adaptation. Understanding the factors at play and actively managing your selection criteria unlocks the true potential of covered calls, navigating you toward maximized profits and controlled risks.

Fundamental and Technical Analysis

Successful investing requires more than just a hunch. It demands a combination of knowledge, strategy, and the right tools at your disposal. In options trading, particularly when considering covered calls, understanding fundamental and technical analysis becomes crucial for confident market navigation.

Fundamental Analysis: Delving into the Company's Core

Fundamental analysis is nothing but peering beneath the surface of a stock. It involves researching a company's financial statements, performance metrics, and industry trends to assess its long-term potential. It builds a strong foundation for your investment decisions.

- **Financial Statements:** Like income statements, balance sheets, and cash flow statements, these reports provide important information about the state of a company's finances, profitability, and debt levels.
- **Company Performance:** Metrics like earnings per share (EPS), revenue growth, and return on equity (ROE) paint a picture of the company's operational efficiency and profitability.

- **Industry Trends:** Understanding the broader economic and industry landscape surrounding a company is essential for gauging its prospects.

Key Fundamental Factors for Covered Calls

When selecting stocks for covered calls, consider these specific fundamental factors:

- **Dividend Yield:** Covered calls can be particularly attractive for stocks with healthy dividend yields, as you earn income from both the premium and the dividends.
- **Earnings Growth:** Companies with consistent and robust earnings growth potential are ideal candidates for covered calls, as they offer the possibility of capital appreciation alongside premium income.
- **P/E Ratio:** While not a standalone metric, a moderate P/E ratio can indicate a company's undervaluation, making it potentially suitable for covered calls with the expectation of price appreciation.

Technical Analysis: Reading the Price Chart's Story

Technical analysis, on the other hand, focuses on the price movements and trends of a stock through charts and indicators. It involves studying the market's pulse to identify your trades' potential entry and exit points.

- **Support and Resistance Levels:** These price zones represent areas where the stock has historically encountered buying or selling pressure, indicating potential turning points.
- **Technical Indicators:** Moving averages, relative strength index (RSI), and Bollinger Bands are just a few examples of tools used

to identify trends, momentum, and potential overbought or oversold conditions.

- **Covered Call Suitability Patterns:** Certain technical chart patterns, like bullish flags or pennants, signal potential price consolidation followed by an upward breakout, making them suitable for covered calls.

Both fundamental and technical analysis are valuable tools, but they shouldn't be used in isolation. Combining them creates a more comprehensive understanding of a stock and the market, ultimately leading to informed investment decisions.

Building Your Selection Criteria

Choosing the right underlying stock for covered calls is crucial for maximizing success. Before diving in, learn to build your selection criteria like a seasoned pro.

Compatibility Check: Key Characteristics for Covered Calls

Your selection criteria is a checklist, ensuring your chosen stock aligns perfectly with a covered call strategy:

- **Liquidity:** High trading volume in both the stock and the options ensures smooth entry and exit, minimizing bid-ask spreads and maximizing your returns.
- **Volatility:** Moderate volatility offers a sweet spot. Highly volatile stocks increase early assignment risk, while low volatility limits premium income. Consider your risk tolerance here.
- **Dividend Considerations:** Choose stocks with healthy dividend yields if you plan to hold long-term. You receive both the premium and the dividend, boosting your overall

return. Remember, dividends are taxed differently than capital gains.

Tailoring Your Criteria: Personal Preferences and Risk Tolerance

Just like a well-fitting suit, your selection criteria should be tailored to your individual needs:

- **Income Generation vs. Capital Appreciation:** Are you prioritizing steady income from premiums, or are you open to higher potential gains through stock price appreciation? It will influence the strike price and expiration you choose.
- **Stability vs. Higher Risk, Higher Reward:** Do you prefer a conservative approach with lower-risk stocks and lower premiums, or are you comfortable with potentially higher returns from riskier assets with higher premiums? Remember, with higher reward comes higher risk.

Additional Tips for Refining Your Criteria:

- **Industry Trends:** Consider the overall health and growth potential of the industry in which the stock operates.
- **Company Fundamentals:** Analyze the company's financial health, profitability, and prospects to assess its long-term viability.
- **Technical Analysis:** Use charts and indicators to identify potential support and resistance levels and understand historical price movements.

Building your selection criteria is an ongoing process. As your investment goals and risk tolerance evolve, so should your criteria.

Continuously research, adapt, and refine your approach to become a master of choosing the right stocks for covered calls.

A Toolkit for Identification: Unveiling the Perfect Stock

Choosing the right stock for a covered call strategy is like a treasure hunt. With countless options scattered across the market landscape, how do you identify the hidden gem that unlocks your desired blend of income generation, capital appreciation, and risk management? This section equips you with the ultimate identification toolkit, empowering you to become a master detective in the case of covered calls.

Screening Tools

What if you had a team of tireless bloodhounds, their noses twitching with anticipation, sniffing out stocks that meet your specific criteria? That's the power of online resources and stock screeners. These platforms act as your digital detectives, meticulously sifting through thousands of companies based on your preferences. Set your parameters, and let the hunt begin.

- **Industry Focus:** Hone in on sectors you understand or find intriguing. Perhaps you're passionate about renewable energy or fascinated by the ever-evolving tech landscape. Targeting specific industries allows you to leverage your existing knowledge and identify potential opportunities you're genuinely interested in.
- **Market Cap Considerations:** Match your stock selection with your investment size and risk tolerance. Large-cap companies offer stability and lower volatility, while venturing into mid or small-cap territory opens doors to potentially higher growth but also carries increased risk. Choose wisely, grasshopper.

- **Dividend Detectives:** Craving steady income streams? Unleash the dividend screeners. These tools unearth companies with attractive payouts, allowing you to double down on your returns by collecting both the premium and the dividend. Dividends are taxed differently than capital gains, so factor that into your calculations.
- **Volatility Gauges:** Navigate the risk-reward spectrum with the help of volatility filters. Moderate volatility offers a sweet spot, providing decent premium income while minimizing the risk of early assignment. If your risk tolerance leans towards the adventurous, consider exploring slightly higher volatility stocks for potentially amplified returns. However, with great volatility comes great responsibility (and potentially significant losses).
- **Technical Tipsters:** Utilize technical indicators like moving averages or RSI to identify potential trends and support/resistance levels. While not foolproof, these tools offer valuable insights into a stock's historical price movements and potential future trajectories.

Popular Screening Tools:

- Finviz
- Yahoo Finance Screener
- Google Finance Screener
- Zacks Investment Research

News and Analysis: Stay Informed, Stay Ahead

Knowledge is the ultimate weapon in any investor's arsenal, and the financial world is no exception. Supplement your screening with trusted sources for financial news and insights, ensuring you stay ahead of the curve:

- **Financial News Powerhouses:** Tap into the expertise of trusted news outlets like Reuters, Bloomberg, and The Wall Street Journal. Get the latest market updates, company announcements, and expert opinions, all conveniently delivered to your fingertips.

- **Investment Research Gurus:** Seek guidance from established research firms like Morningstar, Zacks, and The Motley Fool. Their in-depth analyses, stock ratings, and industry reports provide valuable insights to inform your investment decisions.

- **Industry-Specific Publications:** Dive deeper into the nuances of your chosen sectors by subscribing to industry-specific publications or newsletters. Gain a comprehensive understanding of the latest trends, challenges, and opportunities shaping the landscape, allowing you to make informed choices within your areas of interest.

Don't blindly follow any single source. Cultivate a healthy skepticism, cross-reference information, and develop your own informed opinions based on your research and understanding.

Community and Collaboration

The investment journey doesn't have to be a solitary trek. Leverage the power of online forums and communities to enrich your knowledge and strategies:

- **Learn from the Masters:** Immerse yourself in discussions led by experienced investors. Ask questions, pick up tips from their successes and failures, and learn from their hard-earned wisdom.

- **Share Your Strategies:** Don't be shy. Share your approaches and experiences with the community. Not only will you receive valuable feedback and diverse perspectives, but you'll also contribute to the collective knowledge pool, fostering a collaborative learning environment.
- **Stay Ahead of the Curve:** By engaging with the community, you'll gain access to a constant flow of information, diverse opinions, and real-time discussions about market trends and emerging opportunities. Stay ahead of the curve by tapping into this collective intelligence.

Popular Communities:

- Reddit Investing Subreddits (for example, r/options, r/thetagang)
- Investopedia Forum
- StockTwits

Be mindful and responsible when sharing personal information online. While the investment community offers a wealth of knowledge, prioritize your privacy and maintain a healthy level of skepticism.

Putting Theory into Practice

Translating theoretical knowledge into real-world action requires careful selection of suitable stocks. Here are three practical scenarios and the dissection of the thought process behind each, equipping you to identify your perfect covered call candidate:

Scenario 1: Seeking Stability and Income

Goal: Generate consistent income through premiums while minimizing risk.

Candidate: Consumer Staples Sector (for example, Procter & Gamble (PG))

Reasoning:

- **Stable:** Consumer staples companies offer essential products with consistent demand, leading to predictable revenue and stock prices.
- **Dividend Payers:** Many consumer staples companies distribute attractive dividends, providing additional income on top of the premium.
- **Moderate Volatility:** Lower volatility translates to lower premium income and reduces the risk of early assignment.

Analysis Breakdown:

- **Screeners:** Utilize tools like Finviz or Yahoo Finance to filter for consumer staples stocks with moderate volatility and attractive dividend yields.
- **News and Analysis:** Research the company's financial health, dividend history, and future growth prospects.
- **Technical Analysis:** Analyze charts to identify support and resistance levels, potentially setting your strike price above a key support zone.

Scenario 2: Embracing Volatility for Higher Returns

Goal: Maximize potential capital appreciation while accepting higher risk.

Candidate: Technology Sector (for example, Tesla (TSLA))

Reasoning:

- **High Growth Potential:** Technology companies often experience rapid growth spurts, offering significant upside potential.
- **Higher Premiums:** Due to their volatility, technology stocks offer higher premium income compared to stable companies.
- **Risk Management:** Carefully choose strike prices and expirations to manage the risk of early assignment.

Analysis Breakdown:

- **Screeners:** Focus on high-growth technology companies with moderate to high volatility.
- **News and Analysis:** Pay close attention to industry trends, upcoming product launches, and potential regulatory changes that could impact the stock price.
- **Technical Analysis:** Utilize indicators like Bollinger Bands to identify potential breakout opportunities and set strike prices above resistance levels.

Scenario 3: Sector Selection and Industry Analysis

Goal: Choose a stock within a sector experiencing positive momentum.

Candidate: Healthcare Sector (for example, Abbott Laboratories (ABT))

Reasoning:

- **Industry Trends:** The healthcare sector is expected to experience long-term growth due to aging populations and increasing healthcare needs.
- **Company Fit:** Choose a company within the sector that aligns with your risk tolerance and investment goals.

- **Diversification:** Consider diversifying across different sectors to spread your risk and capture opportunities in various industries.

Analysis Breakdown:

- **Research:** Analyze industry reports and expert opinions to understand the overall sector outlook and identify promising sub-sectors.
- **Company Selection:** Choose a company with strong financials, a competitive advantage, and a track record of innovation within the chosen sub-sector.
- **Community Insights:** Engage with online communities or forums focused on the chosen sector to gain valuable perspectives and insights.

These are just examples, and your specific choices should depend on your individual risk tolerance, investment goals, and market conditions. Always do your research and consider seeking professional advice before making any investment decisions.

You've now reached the culmination of Chapter 3, equipped with the knowledge and tools to make informed stock selections for your covered call strategies. Stock selection is not a static process. As your goals and risk tolerance evolve, so should your criteria.

Continue to refine your selection framework, incorporating lessons learned from experience and market changes. Utilize the resources at your disposal, staying informed with industry trends, company analysis, and expert insights. Above all, practice active management, adapting your portfolio and selection criteria as needed.

Chapter 4

Implementing Covered Call Strategies

You've mastered the fundamentals and explored advanced techniques; now, the moment of truth arrives. It's time to put your knowledge into practice. This chapter is your launchpad, guiding you through executing a covered call strategy confidently and clearly.

You'll discover the practical nitty-gritty, from selecting the right platform and order types to managing your position and navigating potential challenges. Active management is key, and you'll be equipped with the tools and strategies to monitor your positions, adapt to market changes, and make informed decisions throughout your covered call journey.

From Theory to Trade

The allure of covered calls is undeniable, with consistent income generation, built-in risk management, and the flexibility to adapt to market fluctuations. However, translating theoretical knowledge into real-world action requires careful planning and execution. Buckle up because you're about to transform your understanding into your first confident, covered call trade.

Benefits and Risks

Before diving in, refresh your memory on the key benefits and risks associated with covered calls:

Benefits:

- **Steady Income:** Collect premiums consistently, regardless of the stock's price movement within your chosen range.
- **Downside Protection:** Limit potential losses if the stock price falls below your strike price.
- **Capital Appreciation:** Still benefit from price increases within your chosen strike range.

Risks:

- **Early Assignment:** You lose the opportunity for further price appreciation if the stock is called away early.
- **Missed Opportunities:** You forego unlimited upside potential if the stock price rises significantly above your strike price.

Refining Your Stock Selection

By now, you've hopefully mastered the art of choosing the right stock for your covered call strategy (and if not, revisit Chapter 3). Keep these key criteria in mind:

- **Liquidity:** Ensure smooth entry and exit with sufficient trading volume.
- **Volatility:** Moderate volatility offers a balance between premium income and risk.
- **Dividend Considerations:** Choose dividend-paying stocks for additional income.
- **Industry Trends:** Align your selection with promising sectors for potential growth.
- **Company Fundamentals:** Opt for companies with solid financials and long-term prospects.

Step 1: Strike Price and Expiration

This is where things get exciting. Your **strike price and expiration date** significantly impact your potential returns and risks. Here's a deeper look:

Strike Price

The strike price is a line drawn in the sand. It determines the price at which the buyer exercises the option to purchase your shares. Here's the trade-off:

- **Higher Strike = Lower Premium:** You receive less upfront income but retain more potential upside if the stock price rises above the strike. Lower risk of early assignment, as the buyer is less incentivized to exercise the option unless the price significantly surpasses the strike.

- **Lower Strike = Higher Premium:** You earn more upfront income but limit your potential profit and increase the risk of early assignment. The buyer has a greater incentive to exercise the option if the price rises even slightly above the strike, potentially forcing you to sell your shares earlier than anticipated.

Expiration

The expiration date is a ticking clock. It defines the timeframe within which the option can be exercised. Here's how it influences your strategy:

- **Shorter Expiration = Higher Premium (due to time decay):** Ideal for income generation strategies as time value erodes faster the closer you get to expiration. However, this increases the risk of early assignment, especially if the stock price nears the strike price.

- **Longer Expiration = Lower Premium:** Offers more time for potential price movements in your favor, allowing you to capture larger gains if the stock price rises significantly above the strike. However, the premium income is lower due to the slower time decay.

Real-World Examples

If you're considering a covered call on a stock priced at $100 and aiming for a premium of $5, here are two scenarios:

- **Strike: $110, Expiration: One month:** This conservative approach offers lower upfront income but reduces the risk of early assignment. You'll only be assigned if the stock price skyrockets beyond $110 within a month, allowing you to enjoy potential upside within a defined range.
- **Strike: $105, Expiration: Three months:** This aggressive approach offers higher upfront income but comes with a higher risk of early assignment. If the stock price climbs even slightly above $105 within three months, you'll be assigned, potentially limiting your profit potential.

Step 2: Placing Your Trade

Now, translate your carefully crafted strategy into an actual trade. Different order types exist, each with its nuances:

- **Limit Order:** Specifies the exact price you're willing to pay/receive for the option, ensuring you execute the trade at your desired price or better. Ideal for precise execution and controlling costs.
- **Market Order:** Executes the trade immediately at the best available market price, suitable for quick executions but may result in slightly less favorable pricing.

- **Stop-Loss Order:** Automatically sells the option if the price reaches a predetermined level, helping you limit potential losses if the market moves against you.

Essential Details for the Trading Platform:

- **Contract Selection:** Specify the stock symbol, expiration date, and call/put option (you're selling a call in this case).
- **Order Type:** Choose between limit, market, or stop-loss, depending on your preference and strategy.
- **Quantity:** Enter the number of contracts you want to sell (remember, one contract represents 100 shares).
- **Strike Price:** Select the strike price that aligns with your risk tolerance and income goals.
- **Price (for limit orders):** Specify the exact price you're willing to pay/receive per contract.
- **Time in Force (optional):** Set the order duration (for example, good till canceled, day order).
- **Preview and Confirm:** Double-check all details before submitting the order to avoid costly mistakes.

Common Order Entry Mistakes

- **Misunderstanding Order Types:** Ensure you fully understand the difference between limit, market, and stop-loss orders so you don't make any unintended executions.
- **Typos and Incorrect Entries:** Double-check all details, including stock symbol, strike price, and quantity, before submitting the order.
- **Forgetting Expiration Date:** Always pay close attention to the expiration date to avoid missing the deadline for execution.

- **Neglecting Stop-Loss Orders:** Consider using stop-loss orders to manage risk, especially when using aggressive strike prices or shorter expirations.

Executing covered calls involves real financial risk. Practice on a paper trading platform first to gain confidence before using real money. Always consult with a financial advisor before making any investment decisions.

Beyond Execution: Active Management

Congratulations! You've successfully executed your first covered call, but the journey doesn't end there. Active management is the magic ingredient that transforms a simple trade into a strategic approach, maximizing your chances of success in the ever-evolving market landscape. Here are some crucial aspects of post-trade management:

Monitoring and Adjustments

Your covered call position is a living, breathing entity. Just like tending a garden, regular monitoring and adjustments are essential for optimal results. Here's what to keep an eye on:

- **Stock Price Movements:** Track the stock price in relation to your strike price. Are you on course for your desired outcome, or are adjustments needed?
- **Market Volatility:** Changes in volatility impact premium prices. Consider rolling your position if volatility significantly deviates from your initial assumptions.
- **News and Events:** Stay informed about company news, industry trends, and broader market events that could influence the stock price.

Rolling Techniques: Navigating the Expiration Maze

As expiration approaches, you'll face some key decisions. Rolling, which involves closing your current position and opening a new one with different strike and/or expiration dates, offers flexibility to adapt to changing market conditions. Here are some common rolling strategies:

- **Roll for Time:** Extend the expiration date if you believe the stock price has more room to reach your desired profit target.
- **Roll for Strike:** Adjust the strike price up or down based on your updated risk tolerance and profit expectations.
- **Roll for Credit:** When appropriate, close your existing position and open a new one at a higher strike price to collect additional premiums.

Early Assignment: Friend or Foe?

The risk of early assignment is inherent to covered calls. It occurs when the buyer exercises the option to purchase your shares before expiration. While it means you sell your shares at the strike price, potentially limiting your upside, it also frees up your capital and allows you to redeploy it elsewhere. Here's how to handle early assignments:

- **Evaluate the Situation:** Consider if the assigned price fits your initial profit goals and overall investment strategy.
- **Replicate the Strategy:** If you're still bullish on the stock, reopen a covered call position with a new strike price and expiration.
- **Diversify and Redeploy:** Use the assigned capital to diversify your portfolio or explore other investment opportunities.

Closing Trades at the Right Time

Just like entering a trade, exiting at the right time is crucial. Utilize these tools to optimize your closing strategy:

- **Profit Targets:** Set realistic profit targets based on your initial analysis and adjust them based on market changes.
- **Stop-Loss Orders:** Employ stop-loss orders to limit potential losses if the stock price moves against you, especially when using aggressive strike prices.
- **Market Conditions:** Consider broader market sentiment and potential volatility spikes when deciding when to close your position.

Active management is not about micromanaging your position but rather making informed adjustments based on the evolving market landscape and your changing investment goals. Incorporating these strategies into your covered call journey will transform you from a passive observer into an active participant, maximizing your chances of success in the dynamic world of options trading.

Success Stories and Cautionary Tales

Navigating covered calls requires knowledge, discipline, and adaptability. It's time for you to learn through success stories and cautionary tales, allowing you to glean valuable insights for your covered call endeavors.

Case Study 1: Symphony of Success

Meet Sarah: A seasoned investor seeking income generation while maintaining some upside potential. She sets her sights on Company ABC, a stable stock with moderate volatility and a healthy dividend.

The Trade: Sarah opens a covered call on ABC, choosing a strike price slightly above the current market price and an expiration date three months out. It balances premium income with the possibility of capturing some price appreciation.

Active Management: Sarah diligently monitors the stock price and key metrics like volatility. As the stock price dips slightly near expiration, she rolls the call for time, extending the expiration by another month. It allows ABC more time to reach her desired target price.

The Outcome: By expiration, ABC sits comfortably above Sarah's strike price. She collects the premium plus the dividend, enjoying a total return of 15%. Sarah successfully generates income while limiting her downside risk and capturing some upside growth.

Key Takeaways:

- **Strategic Strike and Expiration:** Choosing the right strike and expiration balances income and potential profit.
- **Active Monitoring:** Stay informed and adapt your strategy based on market changes.
- **Rolling Techniques:** Don't be afraid to adjust your position when needed.

Case Study 2: A Cautionary Tale

Meet Mark: An eager investor drawn to the allure of quick profits. He chooses a highly volatile stock, XYZ, hoping for a significant price surge.

The Trade: Mark sets an aggressive strike price far above the current market price, seeking maximum premium income. He opts for a short expiration date, further amplifying his risk-reward profile.

The Pitfalls: Market conditions shift, and XYZ dips below Mark's strike price. He holds on, hoping for a reversal, but the stock continues to decline. Early assignment forces him to sell his shares at a loss, wiping out his premium income and incurring additional capital losses.

Key Takeaways:

- **Understand Volatility:** Misjudging a stock's volatility can lead to disastrous outcomes.
- **Realistic Strike Prices:** Don't chase excessive premiums. Prioritize capital preservation.
- **Mind the Expiration:** Short expirations magnify risk, so choose wisely based on your risk tolerance.

The market is a dynamic teacher, offering both triumphs and tribulations. Studying success stories and learning from cautionary tales will refine your own covered call strategy, minimizing risks and maximizing your chances of achieving your investment goals.

Advanced Techniques for the Seasoned Covered Call Pro

Mastered the basics of covered calls? Your journey doesn't have to end there. Are you ready to dive into advanced techniques? Prepare to unlock greater flexibility, risk management options, and potentially amplified returns.

Spreads and Combinations

A vanilla-covered call is an option that doesn't come with any additional conditions or stipulations, just the right to buy/sell at a certain price by a certain time. Vanilla-covered calls offer stability, but for seasoned players, spreads and combinations unlock a world of possibilities. Consider these powerful tools:

- **Covered Call Spreads:** Pair a short call with a long put or vice versa, creating defined risk parameters and tailoring your income or protection needs.
- **Butterfly Spreads:** Employ multiple calls and puts to create income-generating structures with limited downside risk.

- **Iron Condors:** Utilize four options to create a defined-risk, income-generating strategy with limited upside potential.

These strategies involve greater complexity and require a thorough understanding of option mechanics and risk management.

Quiz

Which of these best describes a covered call spread?
- Selling a call and buying a put at the same strike price.
- Selling a call at a higher strike price than buying a call at a lower strike price.
- Selling a call and buying a put at different strike prices.
- Selling two calls at different strike prices.

Answer: C) Selling a call and buying a put at different strike prices. It creates a defined risk range while generating income or providing protection, depending on the specific combination.

Decision-Making Exercise

You own 100 shares of XYZ stock and believe it will trade within a specific range in the next few months. Would you use a bullish or bearish butterfly spread to achieve this goal?

Hint: A bullish butterfly spread profits if the stock price stays within a range, while a bearish butterfly spread profits if the stock price falls.

Tax Implications

While generating income is enticing, remember the taxman cometh. Covered call profits are treated as short-term capital gains, potentially taxed at a higher rate than other income sources. Consult a tax advisor to fully understand the implications for your specific situation.

Additional Resources

As you navigate the intricacies of advanced strategies, these tools and platforms will become your trusted allies:

- **Advanced Option Analysis Platforms:** Explore platforms like Interactive Brokers or Tastyworks, offering sophisticated tools for analyzing spreads and backtesting strategies.
- **Portfolio Tracking Tools:** Utilize platforms like M1 Finance or Personal Capital to monitor your overall portfolio performance, including covered call positions.
- **Educational Resources:** Immerse yourself in resources like the Options Industry Council (OIC) or Investopedia, expanding your knowledge base and exploring advanced strategies in detail.

Advanced techniques come with increased risk. Always conduct thorough research, understand the mechanics involved, and prioritize risk management before deploying these strategies. Consider seeking professional guidance if needed.

Covered calls offer endless possibilities for customization and adaptation. As you gain experience, experiment with advanced techniques, explore diverse stock selection criteria and refine your risk management approach. Continuous learning and adaptability are your guiding lights in this dynamic market landscape. Embrace the challenges, learn from your experiences, and, most importantly, never stop exploring the potential of covered calls.

Chapter 5

Maximizing Yields and Managing Risks

In the previous chapters, you've laid a solid foundation in covered call strategies, mastering the basics, and exploring advanced techniques. Now, you'll journey towards optimizing your approach to maximize yield while effectively managing risk. This chapter is your roadmap, guiding you through strategies and tools to elevate your covered call game to new heights.

You'll discover the art of selecting high-yielding stocks and explore factors like dividend payouts, volatility, and sector trends. You'll uncover advanced rolling techniques to capture additional profits and adjust your risk exposure as the market unfolds. You'll also unveil the power of portfolio diversification in mitigating risk and ensuring your covered call endeavors contribute to a healthy overall investment strategy.

Rolling Covered Calls and Harnessing Dividends

Are you tired of the standard covered calls? Craving more income, better risk management, and enhanced flexibility? Look no further than the art of rolling covered calls. Buckle up, income seeker, as you go into this powerful strategy, exploring how to roll for profit, manage expiration, adjust risk, and leverage dividends to unlock hidden potential.

Rolling Revealed: A Dynamic Approach

Imagine you've opened a covered call, but the market throws you a curveball. Rolling allows you to proactively adjust your position in response to changing circumstances. Here's how it works:

- **Rolling for Profit:** When the stock price rises above your strike price, and you want to capture further gains, you can roll your call to a higher strike price (often with a later expiration) for a fresh premium.
- **Expiration Management:** As expiration nears, you can roll your call to a later date to avoid early assignment if you're bullish and want to hold the stock longer.
- **Adjusting Risk:** Feeling less bullish? You can roll your call to a lower strike price (often with an earlier expiration) to reduce potential loss while collecting a smaller premium.

Rolling Techniques: Your Toolbox

Now, it's time to look at different rolling styles:

- **Calendar Rolls:** Change the expiration date while keeping the same strike price. It's ideal for managing expiration and capturing potential future price movements.
- **Diagonal Rolls:** Change both the strike price and expiration date, allowing for adjustments in both risk and reward potential.
- **Butterfly Rolls:** More complex strategies involving multiple options to create specific risk-reward profiles.

Calculations Speak Louder Than Words

If you own 100 shares of ABC stock ($50) and sell a covered call with a strike of $55 expiring in 30 days, you collect a premium of $2 per share. After 20 days, the stock price rises to $60. Rolling to a $60 strike with a 60-day expiration earns you another $3 premium. You eventually get assigned at $60, resulting in a total profit of $15 per share ($3 + $2 + $10 capital gain). It translates to a 30% yield enhancement compared to the original $2 premium.

Dividends: Friend or Foe?

Dividends add another layer to the covered call game. When a dividend is declared, the stock price typically drops by the same amount on the ex-dividend date. It affects your covered call premium and overall profitability.

- **Maximizing Income:** Sell covered calls before the ex-dividend date to collect both the premium and the dividend. However, you'll be assigned early if the stock price rises above the strike before the ex-dividend date.
- **Protecting Against Early Assignment:** Consider using cash-secured puts to receive the dividend even if you're assigned early.

Covered Calls on Dividend Champions

Dividend-paying stocks can be excellent candidates for covered calls, especially if the dividends are high and consistent. Remember to factor in the dividend yield when calculating your overall return potential and consider the impact on your risk profile.

Rolling and utilizing dividends are advanced strategies. Always conduct thorough research, understand the risks involved, and consider seeking professional guidance before implementing them. Mastering these techniques will transform your covered call strategies from basic income generators to dynamic tools for maximizing yield, managing risk, and adapting to market changes.

Comprehensive Risk Mitigation Strategies

With their alluring combination of income generation and potential capital appreciation, covered calls have become a popular tool for many investors. However, like any investment strategy, they come with risks. Mastering risk mitigation is crucial to manage this landscape with confidence. Here is a comprehensive arsenal of strategies to empower you to become a proactive risk manager in the covered call arena.

Strike Price: Your Anchor in the Storm

The strike price you select acts as your primary risk management anchor. Choosing a higher strike price reduces your downside risk, but it also limits your potential profit. Conversely, a lower strike price entices you with higher potential gains but exposes you to greater losses if the stock price plummets. It's where strategic selection becomes paramount.

Beyond Strike Price: Expanding Your Risk Mitigation Toolkit

While strike selection lays the foundation, consider these additional tools for enhanced protection:

- **Protective Puts:** These are a safety net for your covered call. Buying a put option with a strike price below your covered call strike acts as this net, limiting your potential losses if the stock price takes a nosedive. It comes at a cost (the premium of the put) but provides valuable peace of mind.
- **Collars:** A collar is a defined risk zone for your position. By selling a covered call and simultaneously buying a put option at a higher strike price, you create a range within which your potential gains and losses are capped. This strategy offers limited upside potential but is ideal for income-focused investors seeking downside protection.

Quantifying the Impact

It's time to bring these concepts to life with a practical example. Imagine you own 100 shares of ABC stock priced at $50.

Scenario 1: You decide to sell a covered call with a strike price of $60. It generates a higher premium, but if the stock price falls to $40, you incur a loss of $10 per share. However, if you had implemented a protective put with a strike of $55, your loss would be limited to the difference between the put strike and the stock price ($5), significantly mitigating your downside risk.

Scenario 2: Seeking maximum potential profit, you opt for a covered call with a strike of $55. While this increases your potential gain, it also exposes you to a larger possible loss if the price dips below $55. In this case, a collar strategy could be beneficial. By selling a covered call at $55 and buying a put at, say, $65, you create a defined risk range, potentially sacrificing some upside in exchange for limiting your downside to $10 per share.

The optimal risk mitigation approach depends on your individual risk tolerance and investment goals. Weighing each strategy's potential rewards and risks is key to making informed decisions.

Diversification: Spreading Your Wings to Reduce Risk

Never put all your eggs in one basket. It's a risky proposition, and the same applies to covered calls. Diversifying your covered calls across different stocks and sectors reduces your risk exposure. Consider:

- **Sector Diversification:** Don't limit yourself to a single industry. Include stocks from various sectors to mitigate the impact of events that might affect specific industries. For instance, include a healthcare stock alongside a technology stock to balance your exposure.

- **Volatility Diversification:** High-volatility stocks offer potentially higher premiums but also have greater risk. Balance them with lower-volatility stocks to create a more stable portfolio.

Taking Control of Your Portfolio

Stop-loss orders are your silent guardians in the market. By automatically selling your position when the price reaches a predetermined level, they help you limit potential losses if the market turns against you. Don't underestimate their power. However, your risk management toolbox doesn't end there. Consider these additional strategies:

- **Delta Hedging:** This involves adjusting your portfolio to maintain a neutral delta, which measures the sensitivity of your position to price changes. It minimizes the impact of stock price fluctuations on your overall portfolio value.
- **Position Sizing:** Don't go all-in on a single covered call. Allocate only a portion of your capital to each position, ensuring your overall portfolio risk exposure remains within your comfort zone.

Risk mitigation is an ongoing process. Regularly monitor your positions, adjust your strategies as needed, and never underestimate the power of diversification and stop-loss orders. Incorporating these strategies and continuously refining your approach will transform you from a passive observer into a confident risk manager.

Advanced Techniques for Covered Call Masters

As your covered call journey progresses, the allure of vanilla strategies might fade, replaced by a yearning for greater control, yield enhancement, and risk management finesse. It's time to unlock the secrets of spreads and combination strategies, unveil the hidden language of the Greeks, and empower you to harness the power of volatility analysis.

Precision with Spreads

What if you had a toolbox bursting with specialized tools, each designed for a specific task? Spreads offer similar versatility, allowing you to tailor your covered call strategy to your precise needs. Here are a few gems in this treasure chest:

- **Covered Call Spreads:** Transcend the limitations of vanilla calls by pairing your short call with a long put or vice versa. This creates a defined risk range, enabling you to generate income or protect your holdings with greater control. Think of it as building walls around your desired outcome, ensuring you stay within your risk tolerance.

- **Butterfly Spreads:** Embrace the intricate beauty of these multi-legged option structures. Employing multiple calls and puts, you craft strategies with limited downside risk while still capturing potential income. Remember it as building a butterfly-shaped tent, sheltering your capital while allowing for controlled upside potential.

- **Iron Condors:** Seeking a defined-risk, income-generating powerhouse? Look no further than the Iron Condor. This four-option strategy establishes a capped upside in exchange for a defined risk and consistent premium income. It's a fortified bridge, providing a safe passage for income generation while limiting your exposure to extreme market movements.

These advanced tools demand a deeper understanding of options mechanics and risk management. Tread carefully, and consider seeking professional guidance if needed.

Options Speak a Secret Language

While stock prices dominate the headlines, the true language of options lies in the Greeks. These cryptic symbols hold the key to understanding how your covered calls react to market movements. Prepare to demystify three crucial ones:

- **Delta:** Delta is the chameleon of options. It reflects how much your option's price changes relative to the underlying stock's price. By understanding Delta, you predict your position's sensitivity to stock movements, ensuring you're not caught off guard by sudden shifts.

- **Gamma:** Gamma is Delta's energetic sibling. It measures how quickly Delta itself changes as the stock price moves. It helps you anticipate how your gains or losses accelerate, allowing you to make informed adjustments to manage your risk exposure.

- **Theta:** Time is money, especially in options trading. Theta represents the relentless decay of your option's value as time passes. By understanding Theta, you can factor in time value when selecting expiration dates and avoid seeing your premiums dwindle before you can capitalize on them.

Mastering these Greeks empowers you to make informed decisions about strike selection, expiration dates, and position adjustments, transforming you from a passive observer to an active participant in shaping your covered call destiny.

Taming the Volatility Beast

Often depicted as a swirling storm cloud, volatility significantly affects option prices. High volatility translates to higher premiums but also amplifies potential losses. As an advanced trader, analyzing volatility becomes your secret weapon for:

- **Strategic Entry Points:** Understand when high volatility presents an opportunity for attractive premiums without excessive risk. Identify calm periods before the storm to stock up on supplies.

- **Dynamic Risk Management:** Use volatility analysis to adjust your strike prices and expiration dates or switch to different spread strategies based on the ever-changing volatility landscape. Adjust your sails based on the wind direction, ensuring you navigate the market currents effectively.

By embracing advanced techniques, deciphering the language of the Greeks, and harnessing the power of volatility analysis, you unlock a new level of control and potential within your covered call strategies. Continuous learning and mindful execution are the keys to navigating this exciting and rewarding path. Step into advanced options trading, write your success story and become a true covered call master.

Chapter 6

Advanced Trading and Beyond

Having mastered the foundational covered call strategies, you now stand at a crossroads. Do you remain within the familiar territory of vanilla calls, content with their steady income stream? Or do you yearn for more significant potential, venturing into advanced trading and beyond?

This chapter is your launching pad, propelling you toward a world of sophisticated strategies, dynamic risk management, and the potential for amplified returns. You'll unearth the intricacies of spreads and combination strategies, empowering yourself to craft custom-built options plays that align with your unique market outlook and risk tolerance.

Exploring New Trading Options for Savvy Investors

While covered calls offer a compelling blend of income generation and downside protection, experienced traders crave the potential for amplified returns. It calls for venturing beyond the familiar and exploring uncovered calls and naked puts, strategies that demand greater understanding and a more active approach to risk management. B

Uncovered Calls

One way to amplify your profit potential is by selling uncovered calls. It means selling the right to buy an asset you don't own. Forgoing the protection of owning the underlying stock helps you pocket potentially larger premiums. Sounds enticing, right? However, remember this comes at a magnified risk:

- **Assignment Risk:** If the stock price rises above your strike price, the buyer can exercise the call, forcing you to sell shares you don't own. It means borrowing the shares to fulfill the obligation, potentially incurring additional costs and margin requirements.
- **Unlimited Loss Potential:** Unlike covered calls, where your loss is capped at the difference between your strike price and the purchase price, your losses with uncovered calls can be significant if the stock price skyrockets.

Taming the Risk: Strategies for Uncovered Calls

So, venturing into uncovered calls demands responsible risk management:

- **Stop-Loss Orders:** Set orders to automatically sell your position if the price goes against you, limiting potential losses.
- **Position Sizing:** Allocate only a small portion of your capital to each uncovered call to mitigate the impact of potential losses on your overall portfolio.
- **Delta Hedging:** Advanced traders use this strategy to partially offset the negative impact of price increases on your position.

Naked Puts: Income Generation with a Twist

Are you intrigued by generating income without owning an asset? Enter naked puts. By selling a put option, you grant the buyer the right (but not the obligation) to sell you the underlying asset at a specific price by a certain date. You collect a premium upfront, but there's a catch:

- **Assignment Risk:** If the stock price falls below your strike price, the buyer can exercise the put, forcing you to buy the asset at the agreed-upon price. It's unfavorable if the price drops significantly.
- **Margin Requirements:** You'll need to have sufficient margin in your account to cover the potential purchase of the asset if assigned.

Managing Naked Put Risks: Tools and Strategies

Just like uncovered calls, responsible risk management is crucial with naked puts:

- **Understand Margin Requirements:** Know exactly how much margin you need to hold to avoid potential account closure due to insufficient funds.
- **Delta Hedging:** Similar to uncovered calls, advanced traders use this technique to manage the delta (price sensitivity) of your position.
- **Careful Strike Selection:** Choose a strike price that aligns with your risk tolerance and potential downside scenario for the underlying asset.

Both uncovered calls and naked puts are advanced strategies with significantly higher risks compared to covered calls. Thorough research, a deep understanding of the mechanics, and responsible risk management are essential before venturing into these territories. Consider seeking professional guidance if needed.

Combining Strategies

Covered calls, while effective, offer limited profit potential and pre-defined risk profiles. However, for adventurous traders, a world of possibilities unfolds when you combine strategies, unlocking a new level of control, income generation, and risk management. It's time to combine covered calls with spreads and other strategies to craft custom-built options for diverse market scenarios.

Spreading Your Wings with Covered Call Spreads:

Have you ever considered combining a covered call with a strategically placed put option? It's where covered call spreads come in, offering greater control and risk management compared to vanilla-covered calls. Here are two popular examples:

- **Bullish Covered Call Spreads:** Want to generate income while limiting your upside potential? Sell a covered call at a higher strike price and simultaneously buy a put option at a lower strike price. It creates a defined risk range, capping your potential gains but also protecting you from significant downside losses.

- **Bearish Covered Call Spreads:** Anticipating a stock price decline? Sell a covered call at a lower strike price and buy a put option at a higher strike price. It generates income while limiting your potential losses if the stock price falls, but it also caps your potential upside gains.

By choosing the right strike prices and expiration dates for both options, you can tailor your covered call spread to your specific market outlook and risk tolerance.

Beyond the Basics: Exploring Further Combinations

Options combinations extend beyond covered call spreads. Consider these advanced strategies:

- **Iron Condors:** Combine four options to create a defined risk, income-generating strategy with limited upside potential. It's ideal for neutral market outlooks or volatility harvesting.

- **Butterfly Spreads:** Employ multiple calls and puts to create a limited-risk, income-generating strategy with targeted upside potential. It's helpful in capturing specific market movements while managing risk.

These strategies involve complex calculations and risk considerations. Thoroughly understand their mechanics and risks before implementing them. Consider seeking professional guidance if needed.

Synergy: The Key to Unlocking Potential

By combining covered calls with spreads and other strategies, you gain the power to:

- **Tailor your Risk Profile:** Define your risk tolerance and create strategies that align with it.
- **Enhance Income Potential:** Generate income from various market scenarios, not just rising prices.
- **Manage Complex Market Dynamics:** Adapt to changing market conditions with more control.

Combining strategies requires a deep understanding of options mechanics, risk management, and market analysis. Start small, research diligently, and prioritize risk management above all else.

A Glimpse into the Future: Where Options Trading Is Headed

Options trading, once a domain of seasoned professionals, is undergoing a metamorphosis thanks to technology and evolving regulations. While the core principles remain, exciting innovations are shaping the future of this dynamic field. It's time to peek into the crystal ball, exploring three key trends pushing the boundaries of options trading:

Technological Advancements: The Rise of the Machines (and Data)

Gone are the days of manual calculations and gut instinct. Technology is revolutionizing options trading through:

- **Algorithmic Trading:** Complex algorithms powered by artificial intelligence (AI) can scan vast datasets, identify lucrative opportunities, and execute trades at lightning speed. It holds immense potential for strategy development, risk management, and efficient execution.

- **Advanced-Data Analysis:** Big data and machine learning are transforming how traders analyze market trends and assess risks. These tools unveil hidden patterns, predict market movements, and assist in identifying optimal entry and exit points.

- **Automated Portfolio Management:** There's a steady rise in software that adjusts your options positions based on real-time market shifts, ensuring your strategies remain in line with your goals. This level of automation will potentially enhance performance and free up valuable time for traders.

However, with great power comes great responsibility. Issues like algorithmic bias, transparency, and potential market manipulation need careful consideration. You must use these tools responsibly and ethically, prioritizing human oversight and sound judgment.

Regulatory Landscape: Adapting to Change

Regulations aim to protect investors and ensure market stability. As innovation advances, regulatory frameworks need to adapt. While specifics are uncertain, potential changes could impact:

- **Leverage Limits:** Adjustments to margin requirements for options trading could affect accessibility and risk profiles.
- **Transparency and Disclosure:** New rules might mandate increased transparency from algorithmic trading platforms.
- **Product Standardization:** Standardized options contracts could simplify trading and enhance accessibility.

Staying informed about evolving regulations is vital for all options traders. Be an active participant in discussions, understand how changes might impact your strategies, and adapt accordingly.

New Developments in Options Products

The options landscape is constantly evolving, with new instruments emerging:

- **Exchange-Traded Options (ETOs):** These pre-packaged options strategies offer investors exposure to specific market movements without needing to select individual options. However, they come with their own set of risks and complexities.
- **Spread Options:** These contracts combine multiple options into one instrument, offering tailored risk profiles and targeted profit potential. Understanding their mechanics and risks is crucial before using them.
- **Exotic Options:** These complex options cater to sophisticated investors seeking to hedge specific risks or capitalize on niche market events. Thorough research and professional guidance are essential before venturing into these instruments.

These new products come with both opportunities and challenges. Carefully evaluate their suitability for your risk tolerance and investment goals before incorporating them into your strategies.

Technology, evolving regulations, and innovative options products are shaping the future of options trading. While these advancements afford exciting possibilities, responsible use and a solid understanding of the underlying principles remain vital.

By adhering to these principles and leveraging the insights gleaned from this chapter, you'll transform your options trading journey from a mere pursuit of income into a strategic path toward achieving your financial aspirations. The market awaits, brimming with opportunities for those who dare to explore and master its intricacies.

Conclusion

"Covered Calls" has equipped you with the knowledge and tools for a rewarding journey in the options trading arena. From demystifying the fundamentals in Chapter 1 to exploring advanced strategies in Chapter 6, this guide has served as your roadmap, empowering you to navigate the complexities of covered calls confidently.

Key Takeaways:

- **Understand the Options Landscape:** Options pose unique ways to generate income, hedge holdings, and speculate on market movements. Covered calls specifically allow you to sell call options on stocks you own, generating premium income while limiting your potential upside.

- **Master the Basics:** Grasping the concepts of strike price, expiration date, intrinsic and extrinsic value, and the Greeks (Delta, Gamma, Theta) is crucial for informed decision-making in covered calls.

- **Strategic Stock Selection:** Choosing the right stocks for covered calls involves considering factors like volatility, liquidity, dividend yield, and your overall investment goals.

- **Execute Effectively:** Learn about various order types, margin requirements, and commission structures to ensure smooth implementation of your covered call strategies.

- **Maximize Yields and Manage Risks:** Explore advanced techniques like spreads and combination strategies to enhance income potential while employing stop-loss orders, delta hedging, and position sizing to manage risk effectively.
- **Delve into Advanced Options:** As your knowledge grows, consider venturing into sophisticated strategies like iron condors and butterfly spreads, but remember to prioritize thorough research and responsible risk management.

Options trading, while potentially lucrative, carries inherent risks. Continuously seek knowledge, understand your risk tolerance, and never hesitate to consult with a financial professional when needed.

This guide would not be complete without your valuable feedback. Please take a moment to share your thoughts. Were the presented strategies practical and easy to understand? Did the book's structure facilitate learning and engagement? Your feedback will help continuously refine and improve this resource, empowering even more individuals to navigate the exciting world of covered calls.

Mastering covered calls is a process, not a destination. Embrace the learning curve, prioritize risk management, and, most importantly, enjoy the journey toward achieving your financial goals.

References

Covered Call Strategy - Meaning, Features, Benefits. (n.d.). Groww. https://groww.in/p/what-is-covered-call-option

Covered Call: Meaning, Objectives, Features & Benefits | 5paisa. (2023, July 28). 5paisa. https://www.5paisa.com/stock-market-guide/derivatives-trading-basics/covered-calls

Covered Call: What Is Covered Call Option Strategy? (n.d.). Angel One. https://www.angelone.in/knowledge-center/futures-and-options/covered-call

Du Plessis, K. (2023, April 20). Covered Call Strategy Guide [Setup, Entry, Adjustment, Exit]. Optionalpha.com. https://optionalpha.com/strategies/covered-call

Options Trading: Basics of a Covered Call Strategy. (2023, May 8). Schwab Brokerage. https://www.schwab.com/learn/story/options-trading-basics-covered-call-strategy

Royal, J. (2023, September 7). What Is a Covered Call? Bankrate. https://www.bankrate.com/investing/covered-call-options-strategy/

Why Use a Covered Call? - Fidelity. (n.d.). Www.fidelity.com. https://www.fidelity.com/learning-center/investment-products/options/why-use-a-covered-call#:~:text=Covered%20calls%20defined